The NFL's Greatest Teams

GREEN BAY PACKERS

Marcia Zappa

Big Buddy Books
An Imprint of Abdo Publishing
www.abdopublishing.com

www.abdopublishing.com

Published by Abdo Publishing, a division of ABDO, PO Box 398166, Minneapolis, Minnesota 55439.
Copyright © 2015 by Abdo Consulting Group, Inc. International copyrights reserved in all countries. No part
of this book may be reproduced in any form without written permission from the publisher. Big Buddy Books™
is a trademark and logo of Abdo Publishing.

Printed in the United States of America, North Mankato, Minnesota.
042014
092014

Cover Photo: ASSOCIATED PRESS.
Interior Photos: ASSOCIATED PRESS.

Coordinating Series Editor: Rochelle Baltzer
Contributing Editors: Bridget O'Brien, Sarah Tieck
Graphic Design: Michelle Labatt

Library of Congress Cataloging-in-Publication Data

Zappa, Marcia, 1985-
  Green Bay Packers / Marcia Zappa.
     pages cm. -- (The NFL's greatest teams)
  ISBN 978-1-62403-361-2
 1. Green Bay Packers (Football team)--History--Juvenile literature. I. Title.
  GV956.G7Z36 2015
  796.332'640977561--dc23
                                          2013048632

Contents

A Winning Team

The Green Bay Packers are a football team from Green Bay, Wisconsin. They have played in the National Football League (NFL) for more than 90 years.

The Packers have had good seasons and bad. But time and again, they've proven themselves. Let's see what makes the Packers one of the NFL's greatest teams.

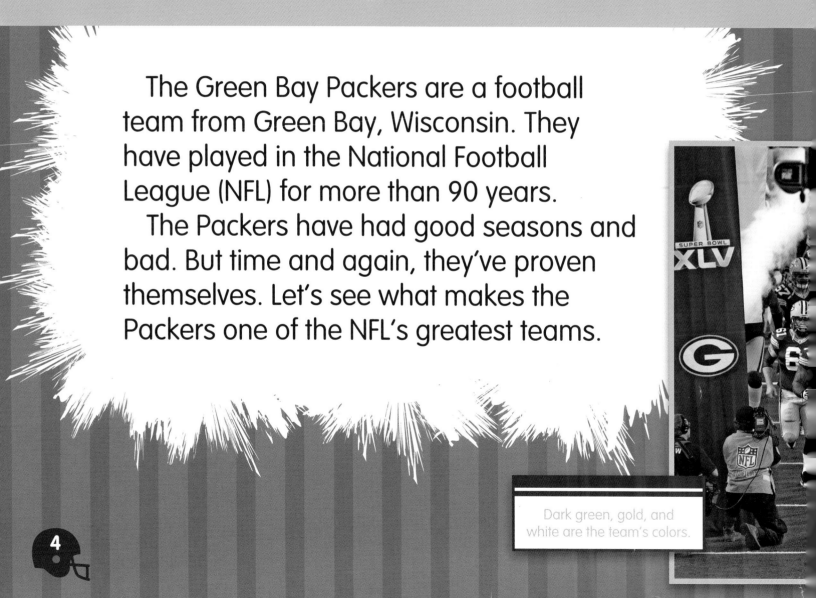

Dark green, gold, and white are the team's colors.

Touchdown

The Packers have won 13 NFL championships. That is more than any other team!

Aaron Rodgers became the team's starting quarterback in 2008.

5

League Play

   The NFL got its start in 1920. Its teams have changed over the years. Today, there are 32 teams. They make up two conferences and eight divisions.

   The Packers play in the North Division of the National Football Conference (NFC). This division also includes the Chicago Bears, the Detroit Lions, and the Minnesota Vikings.

Team Standings

The NFC and the American Football Conference (AFC) make up the NFL. Each conference has a north, south, east, and west division.

The Vikings (*above*), the Bears, and the Lions are all rivals of the Packers. Beating rival teams is important to players and fans.

RIVALRY SINCE 1921

Kicking Off

The Packers became a team in 1919. The team was set up by George Calhoun and Earl "Curly" Lambeau. Lambeau played for the team and was its first head coach.

At first, the Packers struggled to make money. So in 1923, the team became a nonprofit corporation. It was paid for by people in the Green Bay area.

Time Out

The Packers is the only publicly owned team in the NFL. Fans are very proud to be team owners.

Lambeau worked for a packing company. It helped pay for the team during its early years. So, the team was named the "Packers" for it.

9

Highlight Reel

The Packers soon became a strong team. They were the NFL champions in 1929, 1930, 1931, 1936, 1939, and 1944. They struggled for a bit. Then, they became champions again in 1961, 1962, and 1965.

In 1967, the Packers played in the very first Super Bowl. They beat the Kansas City Chiefs 35–10. The next year, they won the Super Bowl for a second time. They beat the Oakland Raiders 33–14.

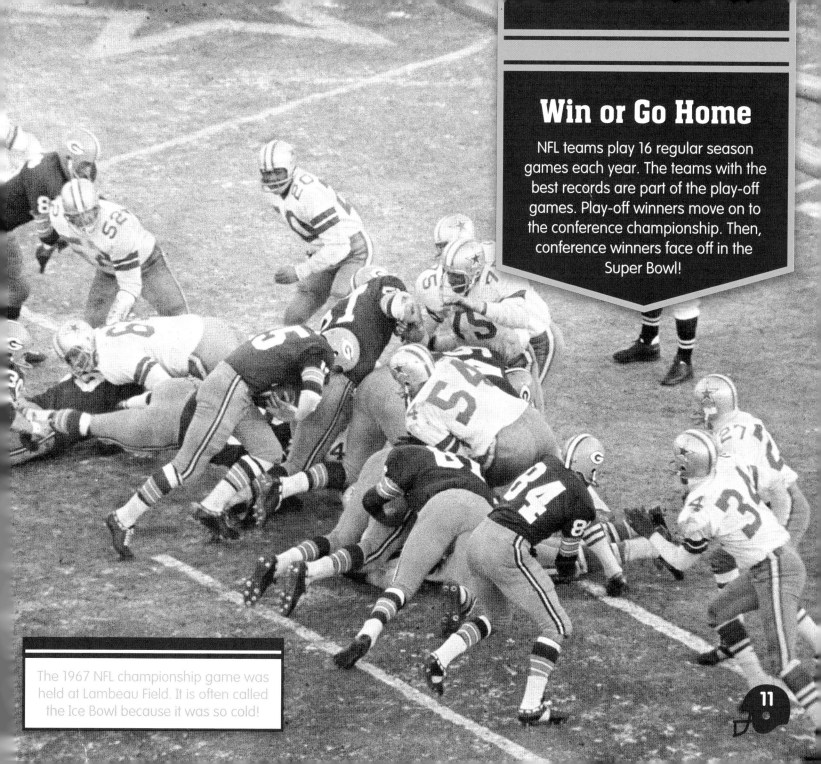

Win or Go Home

NFL teams play 16 regular season games each year. The teams with the best records are part of the play-off games. Play-off winners move on to the conference championship. Then, conference winners face off in the Super Bowl!

The 1967 NFL championship game was held at Lambeau Field. It is often called the Ice Bowl because it was so cold!

In 1992, coach Mike Holmgren and quarterback Brett Favre joined the Packers. They led the team to the play-offs six years in a row.

In 1997, the Packers made it back to the Super Bowl. They beat the New England Patriots 35–21. The team returned to the Super Bowl the next year. But, they lost to the Denver Broncos 31–24.

The Packers were a strong team in the 2000s. In 2011, they played in their fifth Super Bowl. They beat the Pittsburgh Steelers 31–25.

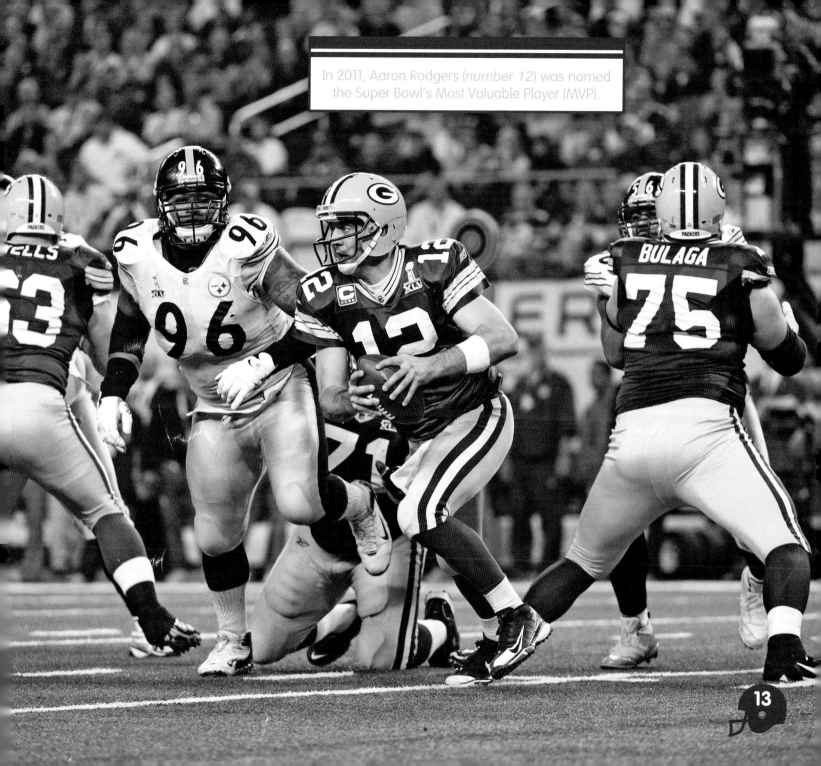

In 2011, Aaron Rodgers (*number 12*) was named the Super Bowl's Most Valuable Player (MVP).

Halftime! Stat Break

Team Records

RUSHING YARDS
Career: Ahman Green, 8,322 yards (2000–2006, 2009)
Single Season: Ahman Green, 1,883 yards (2003)
PASSING YARDS
Career: Brett Favre, 61,655 yards (1992–2007)
Single Season: Aaron Rodgers, 4,643 yards (2011)
RECEPTIONS
Career: Donald Driver, 743 receptions (1999–2012)
Single Season: Sterling Sharpe, 112 receptions (1993)
ALL-TIME LEADING SCORER
Ryan Longwell, 1,054 points (1997–2005)

Famous Coaches

Earl "Curly" Lambeau (1919–1949)
Vince Lombardi (1959–1967)

Championships

EARLY CHAMPIONSHIP WINS:
1929, 1930, 1931, 1936, 1939, 1944, 1961, 1962, 1965

SUPER BOWL APPEARANCES:
1967, 1968, 1997, 1998, 2011

SUPER BOWL WINS:
1967, 1968, 1997, 2011

Pro Football Hall of Famers & Their Years with the Packers

Herb Adderley, Cornerback (1961–1969)
Tony Canadeo, Halfback (1941–1944, 1946–1952)
Willie Davis, Defensive End (1960–1969)
Forrest Gregg, Tackle/Guard (1956, 1958–1970)
Arnie Herber, Quarterback (1930–1940)
Clarke Hinkle, Fullback (1932–1941)
Paul Hornung, Halfback (1957–1962, 1964–1966)
Robert "Cal" Hubbard, Tackle (1929–1933, 1935)
Don Hutson, End (1935–1945)
Henry Jordan, Defensive Tackle (1959–1969)
Earl "Curly" Lambeau, Founder/Coach (1919–1949)
James Lofton, Wide Receiver (1978–1986)

Vince Lombardi, Coach (1959–1967)
John "Blood" McNally, Halfback (1929–1933, 1935–1936)
Mike Michalske, Guard (1929–1935, 1937)
Ray Nitschke, Middle Linebacker (1958–1972)
Jim Ringo, Center (1953–1963)
Dave Robinson, Linebacker (1963–1972)
Bart Starr, Quarterback (1956–1971)
Jim Taylor, Fullback (1958–1966)
Reggie White, Defensive End (1993–1998)
Willie Wood, Safety (1960–1971)

Fan Fun

NICKNAMES: The Pack, The Green and Gold
STADIUM: Lambeau Field
LOCATION: Green Bay, Wisconsin
TEAM SONG: "Go! You Packers! Go!"

Coaches' Corner

Earl "Curly" Lambeau was the first head coach of the Packers. He coached the team until 1949. Lambeau led the team to the NFL championship six times.

In 1959, Vince Lombardi took over the Packers. His focus on hard work and winning helped the team succeed. Lombardi led the Packers to five NFL championships and two Super Bowl wins.

Playbook

Lambeau helped improve the NFL. He was the first coach to hold daily team practices, use pass patterns, and fly to away games.

Mike McCarthy became the head coach for the Packers in 2006.

VINCE LOMBARDI TROPHY

NFL

After Lombardi died in 1970, the Super Bowl trophy was named for him.

17

Star Players

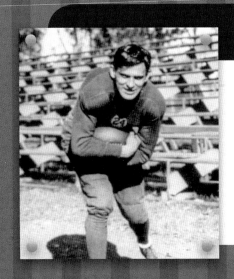

John "Blood" McNally HALFBACK (1929–1933, 1935–1936)

John "Johnny Blood" McNally helped the Packers win many early championships. His great speed made him good at rushing and receiving. He was also skilled at passing, punting, and defense. In 1963, he became one of the first players in the Pro Football Hall of Fame.

Don Hutson END (1935–1945)

Don Hutson was one of the NFL's first great receivers. While with the Packers, Hutson led the league in scoring five times. He was named the NFL's MVP in 1941 and 1942. When he retired, Hutson held 18 NFL records!

Bart Starr QUARTERBACK (1956–1971)

Bart Starr became the team's starting quarterback in 1959. He led the team to many early championships. Starr was named the NFL's MVP in 1966. In 1967 and 1968, he led the Packers to win the first two Super Bowls. Starr was named the MVP of both games!

Reggie White DEFENSIVE END (1993–1998)

Reggie White was a powerful defensive end. He helped the Packers win the Super Bowl in 1997 by sacking New England's quarterback three times. When White retired, he had 198 sacks. That was the most in the NFL until 2003.

Brett Favre QUARTERBACK (1992–2007)

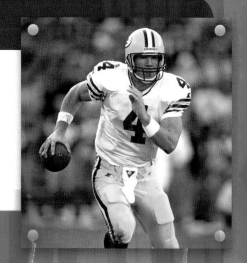

Brett Favre played 255 games for the Packers. That is more than any other player. He was named the NFL's MVP three times. In 1997, he led the Packers to their third Super Bowl win. During his NFL career, Favre broke many passing records.

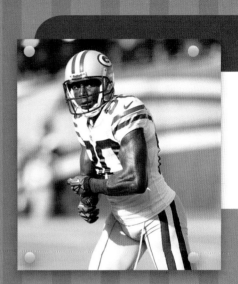

Donald Driver WIDE RECEIVER (1999–2012)

Donald Driver played for the Packers his whole career. During this time, he had seven 1,000-yard seasons. And, he caught a total of 743 passes for 10,137 yards. That is more than any other Packer.

Aaron Rodgers QUARTERBACK (2005–)

Aaron Rodgers was drafted by the Packers in 2005. He became the team's starting quarterback in 2008. In 2011, Rodgers led the Packers to win the Super Bowl. He was named the game's MVP.

Lambeau Field

The Packers play home games at Lambeau Field. It is in Green Bay, Wisconsin. Just more than 100,000 people live there. That makes it the smallest US city to have a major professional sports team.

Lambeau Field opened in 1957. It has been improved many times over the years. It can hold about 73,000 people.

Running Out the Clock

Lambeau Field is the oldest NFL stadium in the United States.

Lambeau Field was named for the Packers' first coach after he passed away in 1965. It was first called City Stadium.

Lambeau Field is sometimes called the Frozen Tundra. It can be very cold and snowy there in the winter!

Cheeseheads

Wisconsin is known for making cheese. So, Packers fans are often called Cheeseheads. Many cheer on their team by wearing large, yellow hats in the shape of cheese.

When a Packer makes an important play, he often jumps into the stands. This is called the Lambeau Leap. The Leap started in 1993 after a touchdown by LeRoy Butler.

Fans get excited to cheer on players during the Lambeau Leap.

The first Cheesehead hat was made in 1987. It was made out of a couch cushion.

Final Call

The Packers have a long, rich history. They have been the NFL champions more than any other team. Even during their losing seasons, true fans have stuck with them. Many believe that the Green Bay Packers will remain one of the NFL's greatest teams.

On the first day of training camp, Packers ride kids' bikes to the practice field. Lombardi started this fun practice.

Through the Years

1919

Earl "Curly" Lambeau and George Calhoun form a football team.

1921

The Packers join the American **Professional** Football Association. Later, this league is named the NFL.

1923

After struggling to make money, the Packers become a **nonprofit corporation**. They are supported by people in the Green Bay area.

1929

The Packers win their first NFL **championship**.

1936

The Packers are part of the first NFL **draft**. Their first pick is guard Russ Letlow.

1957

City Stadium opens. It is renamed Lambeau Field in 1965.

1967

The Packers win the first Super Bowl.

2011

The Packers win the Super Bowl. They become the NFL **champions** for a record 13th time.

1960

Paul Hornung scores 176 points in one season. This was an NFL record until 2006.

1993

LeRoy Butler invents the Lambeau Leap.

2007

Brett Favre breaks the NFL record by throwing his 421st touchdown pass.

1995

Lambeau Field becomes the team's only home field. Before this, they had played four home games a year in Milwaukee.

Postgame Recap

1. How many NFL championships have the Packers won?
   A. 13   B. 15   C. 11

2. Who was the first coach of the Green Bay Packers?
   A. Vince Lombardi   B. George Calhoun   C. Earl "Curly" Lambeau

3. Name 3 of the 22 Packers in the Pro Football Hall of Fame.

4. How did the Packers solve their early money problems?
   A. They drafted new players and became a better, more popular team.
   B. Vince Lombardi became their new owner.
   C. They became a nonprofit corporation supported by people in the Green Bay area.

Glossary

career work a person does to earn money for living.

champion the winner of a championship, which is a game, a match, or a race held to find a first-place winner.

draft a system for professional sports teams to choose new players. When a team drafts a player, they choose that player for their team.

nonprofit corporation a group that exists for a purpose other than to make a profit.

professional (pruh-FEHSH-nuhl) working for money rather than only for pleasure.

retire to give up one's job.

Websites

To learn more about the NFL's Greatest Teams, visit **booklinks.abdopublishing.com**. These links are routinely monitored and updated to provide the most current information available.

Index